MODERN AMERICANA

MAX HUMPHREY
WITH CHASE REYNOLDS EWALD

PHOTOS BY
CHRISTOPHER DIBBLE

GIBBS SMITH
TO ENRICH AND INSPIRE HUMANKIND

First Edition
25 24 23 22 21   5 4 3 2 1

Text © 2021 Max Humphrey and Chase Reynolds Ewald
Photographs © 2021 Christopher Dibble

Published by
Gibbs Smith
P.O. Box 667
Layton, Utah 84041

1.800.835.4993 orders
www.gibbs-smith.com

Designed by Rita Sowins / Sowins Design
Custom cover fonts by Paige Thammavong

Gibbs Smith books are printed on either recycled, 100% post-consumer waste,
FSC-certified papers or on paper produced from sustainable PEFC-certified
forest/controlled wood source. Learn more at www.pefc.org.
Printed and bound in China

Library of Congress Control Number: 2020944737
ISBN: 978-1-4236-5739-2

THOUGHTS ON MODERN AMERICANA
– MAX HUMPHREY –

1 DESIGN IS NOSTALGIA

When I was a kid growing up in New England, my parents would drag me to antique malls on the weekends. If I was lucky, there would be a pinball machine in the lobby, because otherwise it was the last thing in the world I wanted to be doing on a Saturday in the summertime. I've read about interior designers who had subscriptions to *Elle Decor* when they were in kindergarten, but I wasn't that kid. I was in the woods blowing up my G.I. Joes and playing video games. Fast forward to now and my favorite thing to do on the weekend is drag my family to junky antique malls. Someone said that interior design is autobiography. For me, it's nostalgia.

2 DIY

I was the bass player in a punk band when I was in my early twenties. We did everything ourselves, from booking our own shows to hand screen-printing our merch T-shirts. That philosophy has carried over into my approach to design. We've gotten used to hiring people to do things that we can do ourselves, but you can paint your own bedroom and watch YouTube videos to learn how to rewire a vintage lamp. You get more value out of things when you do them yourself, and it makes you appreciate it more when you actually do hire a professional.

3 SIGNS OF LIFE

In my work creating campaigns as an art director and stylist for furniture catalogs, it's never about the thing—the chair itself or the coffee table. It's about telling a story. That's why I like to put signs of life in all my photos. It should look like someone just walked out of the room and then the camera snapped a pic. Do you read design magazines and think people actually live like that? Where are the empty juice boxes? Where's the dog bowl? Where's the STUFF?

4 LEARN BY DOING

I'm self-taught and I learned by doing. You can put in the 10,000 hours, but it doesn't have to be in a classroom. It can be spent in your own living room, arranging and rearranging, painting and repainting. When I walked into the interview for my first job in interior design, I didn't have a resume or a portfolio or a degree, but I was hungrier than anyone else there. I would eat and sleep interior design. I read every book, magazine and design blog, and I would practice in my own apartment so that by the time I entered the field, I was ready.

5 HURRY UP AND WAIT

People are used to "buy it now" and grocery deliveries by drone, but good design takes time. I get calls from people all the time who just bought a house or are remodeling and expect me to install furniture in a few weeks. Interior design is not like it is on TV where there's a big reveal at the end with scented candles burning. Most of my projects take many months, some take many years, and the really good ones never actually end.

6 FORM & FUNCTION

When I'm designing a home for new clients, I like to first get to the root of how they live. Are they homebodies who prioritize Netflix and chilling with family? Do they entertain a lot and need a table that can seat twenty people—or can we get rid of the dining room and make it a ping-pong play space instead? Do they have half a dozen border collies (or toddlers) and need indestructible upholstery? I don't design rooms that are too precious to hang out in, even in a fancy house.

7 COLOR OUTSIDE THE LINES

The first step in designing a room is thinking about a color palette, and that can be daunting. Nature can be a great source of inspiration. There's a blue jay hopping across my lawn as I type this. When in doubt, look in your closet and see what colors pop up again and again. I wear blue jeans and army jackets every day, and there's a lot of blue and green in this book.

8 MODERN AMERICANA AT HOME

Good design is right outside your door, whether you're referencing the surroundings or supporting local businesses and makers. In Portland, I can buy a piece of Oregon walnut from a family-owned slab yard and have it made into a table by a local furniture builder.

9 BE YOURSELF

There's a quote on my website, "Style is knowing who you are, what you want to say, and not giving a damn." The best compliment I get is when someone says they saw a picture of a room in a magazine or online and they knew I designed it before reading the caption. It's like when you turn on the radio and you hear "She was an American girl raised on promises" and you know it's Tom Petty from the first note. There's no one else it could be.

10 ELEMENTS OF MODERN AMERICANA

This book is organized by design element rather than by project. It is as much about style and styling as it is about interiors. *Modern Americana* is meant to be read front to back, back to front, from the middle out or upside down. Don't follow my rules—or anyone else's!

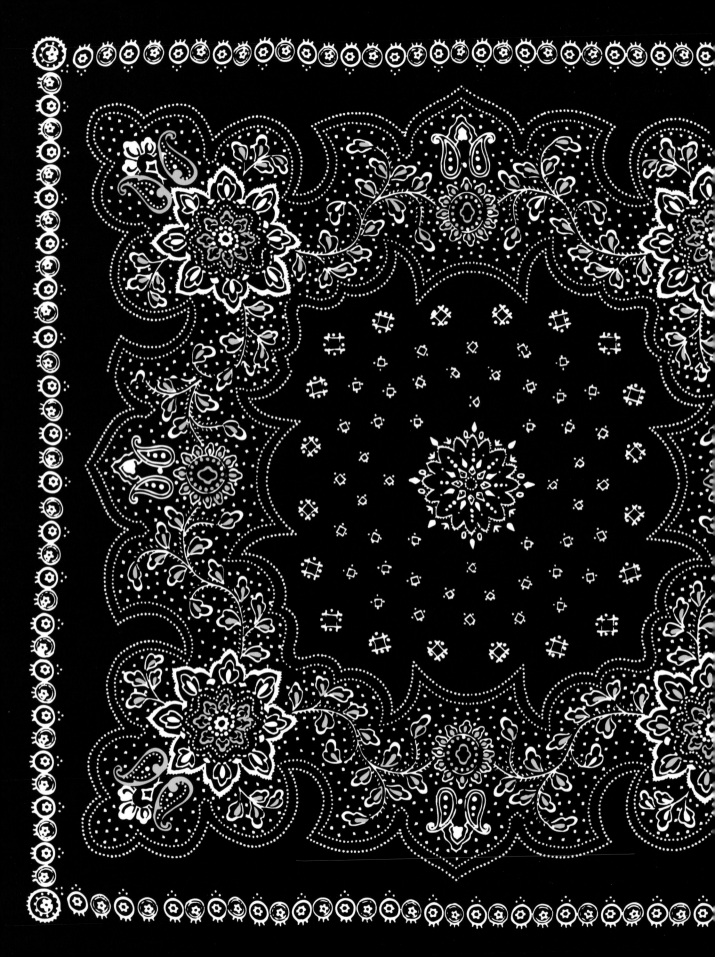

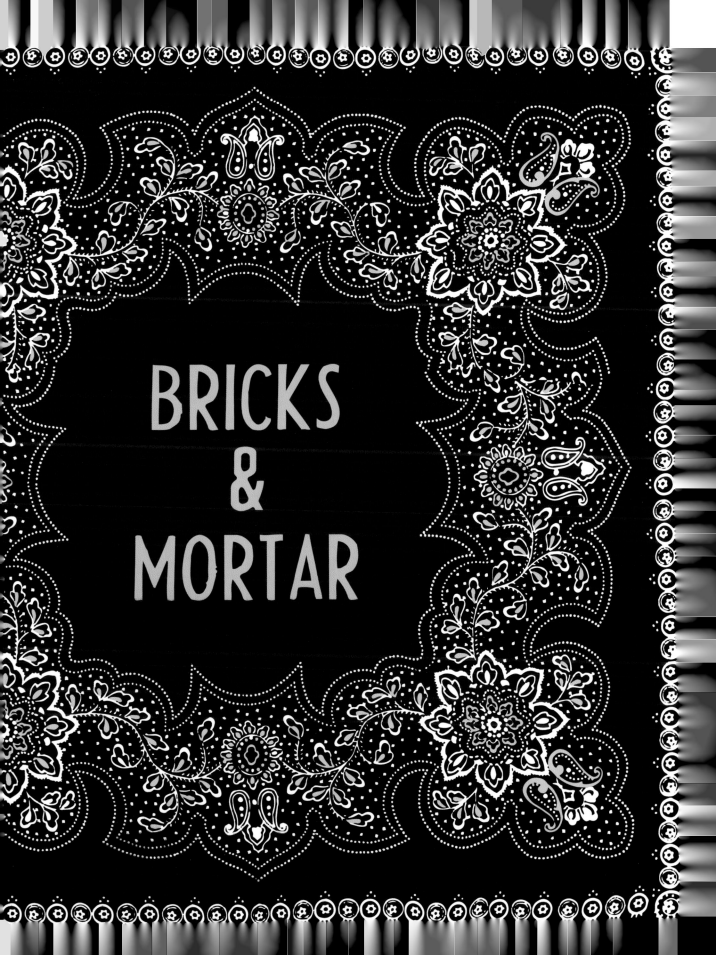

BRICK

I'M FROM NEW HAMPSHIRE, where there was brick everywhere, and then I went to college in Boston, where there was brick everywhere, and then I moved to L.A. and didn't see any for twenty years. There's something modern about white-painted brick, while red brick has an old-school vibe. ★ My former loft was in a 1920s building that had been a Heinz tomato ketchup factory. There was one red-brick wall. I would have painted it, but I wouldn't have gotten my security deposit back, so I learned to love the red brick.

The chair, sofa, hairpin side table and green-painted Sculptura chair are all 1950s vintage pieces, though not all the same style. Hairpin tables are iconic midcentury Americana. A crate flipped upside down makes a quick and easy surface.

BRASS

BRASS is a favorite metal finish for Americana-themed spaces because you can dress it up or down. ★ I particularly like an unlacquered brass finish that starts to show signs of age as it develops verdigris and becomes patinated. I like the fact that it transforms, as opposed to metal finishes that never change. It's a badge of honor, like a wallet outline in the back pocket of a pair of jeans you've been wearing forever. ★ Brass on brass looks cool, but you can mix it with black or silver finishes as well. For people who don't like that living-finish look, you can have brass on surfaces you don't touch every day, such as light fixtures, and use black or chrome finish on things you do touch, like drawer hardware and faucets.

OPPOSITE: In this basement bath remodel, the faucet is from Watermark, a Brooklyn-based plumbing company. The vanity is from Rejuvenation.

ABOVE: The brass pendant light, manufactured in Charleston, South Carolina, by Urban Electric Company, plays off the brass sabots on the custom kitchen island in a home I designed for a family in Bend, Oregon. The finishes don't all match; we used polished nickel on the Waterworks faucet.

CHROME

There's something so 1950s diner about chrome.
I think it looks better mismatched than as a full dinette
set. It's retro modern at its finest.

HEXAGONS

Hexagons are a favorite tile for bathrooms, and if you're using subway tiles on the walls, a hexagon is great for the floor because it's a different shape. ★ These tiles were popularized in the 1920s and '30s but still look just as fresh today in a modern setting. Using them in a contrasting black-and-white pattern is the classic application, but if you use them monochromatically, they can look even more contemporary.

The hexagons I used on the floor of the colorful striped guest bathroom are two inches, so they're small enough to go in the shower as well as in the main space of the bathroom. In the one above, I used the big hexagon from Tempest Tileworks in Portland for the tub and vanity area but switched to a much smaller hexagon in the shower. I used light gray grout in both spaces. It's easier to clean and makes for less white-and-black contrast.

PENNY
ROUNDS

PENNY ROUND TILES come in sheets. For this bathroom I picked black and white penny rounds from Ann Sacks, and my tile installer cut the sheets to size and fused them together to create stripes. They go up the sides of the shower curb for an extra little stripey bonus.

SUBWAY TILES

SUBWAY TILES are found in both classic and contemporary homes. It's nice that something that's been around since the Victorian era can be done in a modern way today. ★ Subway tiles are easy to clean, especially if you use gray grout. They're fun to put your stamp on since there are lots of colors and sizes. I usually don't have the restraint to do an all-white kitchen or bathroom. ★ The most recognizable tile pattern is running bond, but subway tile looks really modern when stacked one atop another or run vertically. ★ You can buy handmade tile or tile made out of marble, but you can also get it for a dollar a square foot. I use subway tile on vertical surfaces in kitchens and bathrooms: on walls, backsplashes, shower walls and curbs. In a kitchen it looks cool going all the way to the ceiling. I typically don't use it on horizontal surfaces. Tile countertops were a hallmark of homes in the '60s and '70s, but they're a pain to clean.

The stair railing is custom and the wooden arrow is from Aurora Mills Architectural Salvage. A built-in bookcase in the entry displays books and collectibles.

STEEL
& IRON

INTO THE WOODS

WALL TREATMENTS

In my own home, I installed pine tongue-and-groove paneling on the walls and cedar on the ceiling.

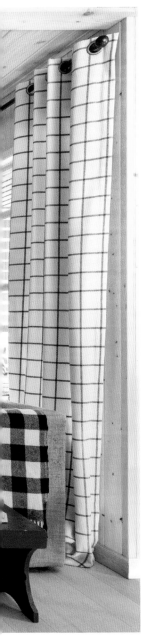

I HAVE AN AVERSION TO DRYWALL. I like the look, feel and texture of wall paneling. ⭐ When possible, I use beadboard, tongue and groove, shiplap or board-and-batten to add architectural interest. These are versatile materials that can go preppy or nautical or modern or industrial, depending on the setting and how they're applied. Running them vertically draws the eye up and makes the ceilings look higher. It's easy to install yourself, especially if it's wainscot height. You can buy paneling that clicks together or comes in sheets. If you choose satin or semigloss paint, it's easy to wipe off dirty handprints when your kid runs through with peanut butter-and-jelly hands.

Vertical shiplap
provides an opportunity
for a gallery art wall
surrounding the TV in
a basement media room.

In this Boston bathroom, the pesky contractor bowed down to building codes and wouldn't install a chandelier over the bathtub. So I hung a $50 disco ball.

PLYWOOD

PLYWOOD is a utilitarian and universal material that's cheap and easy to work with and smells good too. ✶ I like adding midcentury furniture to more traditional Americana spaces. A whole suite can tend to look like the set of *Mad Men*, but when combined with some other elements, it becomes an interesting mix. ✶ Molded plywood furniture was popularized by Charles and Ray Eames, who designed their iconic plywood lounge chair during World War II. While he worked as a set painter with MGM to pay the bills, she perfected their design in the spare room of their Venice, California, apartment. ✶ Plywood can be used for large-scale projects, such as cladding the roof and walls of a surf shack, or for small projects like bookshelves or a soapbox derby car. I used it for the cabinetry in my own kitchen and applied a lacquer finish so it's easy to clean tomato sauce stains.

Cutout circles add quirky interest to these 1950s–'60s-era stackable midcentury chairs. The moon print is from Juniper Print Shop.

Brass hardware from Schoolhouse Electric dresses up the plywood cabinetry in my kitchen.

34

PINE

Pine can be used as a building material or for making furniture or as an interior wall cladding. It's inexpensive and lightweight, and you can either paint it or let it patina. ★ Pine has knots and graining, so each piece looks different. Your vintage pine dresser doesn't look the same as my vintage pine dresser.

In this beach house on the Oregon coast, Portland architects Beebe Skidmore opened up our clients' 1970s time capsule by vaulting the ceilings and installing the wraparound windows and bench seat. I added family-friendly fabrics and furniture.

37

BARN DOORS

BARN DOORS serve two important purposes. The first is that they're functional space savers when you don't have room for a door to swing open. Putting the door on a track means you won't eat into the next room's furniture arrangement. ★ In this beach house bedroom, there wasn't an obvious wall for the bed, so I decided to float it in the middle of the room, with a view of the ocean. There wasn't space for swinging doors to the bathroom and closet, so I had a single track fabricated for two doors to slide open, with just enough room to walk behind the bed. The other equally important function is that barn doors look awesome.

RECLAIMED WOOD

The wall cladding in this room is from Salvage Works of Portland. They source reclaimed wood from old barns in the Pacific Northwest. This particular treatment is a mix of cedar and redwood.

SITTING, SNOOZING, STANDING AROUND

PAINTED FURNITURE

PAINTED FURNITURE is a category I can't say no to. It's a great way to get a pop of color in a space. There's nothing fancy about these pieces of furniture, and there's no stopping you from repainting a chair, desk, cabinet or outdoor furniture and giving it new life. You can paint vintage wood or metal outdoor furniture to modernize it. If the color doesn't suit, you can do it again. ★ When you find the old stuff, it's unmistakable. For me, the chippier the better. Gapping, cracks and visible nails all lend character. I like being able to see layers of paint. I might find a painted chair or desk or table and it's got the one color you can see but it's not just brown beneath; it might have been painted red then black then blue then green. You can see the layers and the lives this piece has had. All these pieces have a history that you'll never know, but you make up your own story for them.

This is an ode to the times when you come home with one random vintage chair, until you have enough for a whole dinner party.

STOOLS
& BENCHES

In this kitchen, oak-and-leather counter stools surround the plywood island, while the vintage milking stool offers a boost to the kids so they can wash their hands at the farmhouse sink.

I bought the cast-iron tub on Craigslist and it was no fun to transport. A vintage Oregon flag serves as a makeshift shower curtain.

BATHTUBS

THERE'S NOTHING QUICK OR PRACTICAL ABOUT A BATHTUB, and that's why they're so appealing. You have to draw a bath, wait for it to fill up, then let some water out when you realize it's too hot. ★ There's something elemental about bathtubs and hot water. Every culture and every religion has a bathing ritual.

I added a mattress-style cushion to the floating concrete fireplace hearth in this mountain home as a way to soften some of the heavier materials.

WINDOW SEATS

WHO DOESN'T LOVE A WINDOW SEAT?

Window seats need to be comfy, and it's nice if they're long enough to take a nap on. They're a good vessel for throw pillows and a place to add texture, color and pattern. Cats love them. In fact, my cat gets way more use out of mine than I do.

BUTTERFLY CHAIRS

BUTTERFLY CHAIRS ARE CASUAL. They force you to relax. They're great inside as sculptural accents in a modern room but also comfortable on the porch. You can change the cover to instantly transform a room. They're good as reading chairs and they're great in a kid's room. For a little kid, they're almost like hammocks. ★ I like that you have to climb into a butterfly chair. It's not a passive experience; you have to be an active participant in sitting in this chair. And once you're in it, you're in it. You need a friend to get you out—or you just fall out.

BUNK BEDS

People love bunk beds, and when I work on new builds or renovations everyone wants them. But they're a feat of spatial engineering. I do as much as I can on paper, but I was at this house with blue painter's tape taping off a whole 3D plan, making sure people would have enough room on the top and still not hit their heads on the bottom. The niche has to be in the right spot; the junction boxes for the sconces have to be determined really early on. There's no wiggle room.

ROCKING & SWINGING

ROCKING CHAIRS are most at home on a porch. They always make me think of the Everly Brothers version of "Rockin' Alone (In An Old Rocking Chair)." ☆ The thing about rocking chairs is that you're moving but not going anywhere. ☆ Additionally, a midcentury hanging chair, a rope swing or a hammock is another way to bring the outside in. The hanging mechanism adds a vertical element that draws your eye up.

VINTAGE RUGS

This is a 1920s house that I decorated for a young family expecting their first baby. The clients had modern taste but bought this traditional home with some cool original details, like pocket doors, leaded windows and original built-ins. It's sometimes fun to paint pass-through rooms a darker color, like the dining room in the background. The rug is antique Moroccan from Kat and Maouche. The more baby spit-up it gets on it, the better it looks.

THE MORE BEAT-UP, THE BETTER THE RUG. IF IT'S LASTED THIS LONG, IT'S GOING TO LAST ANOTHER HUNDRED YEARS.

The rug dealer tried to talk me out of buying this one because it was damaged, but the truth is, I would have paid extra for it.

OPPOSITE: Stained glass windows + rockin' rug = 😊

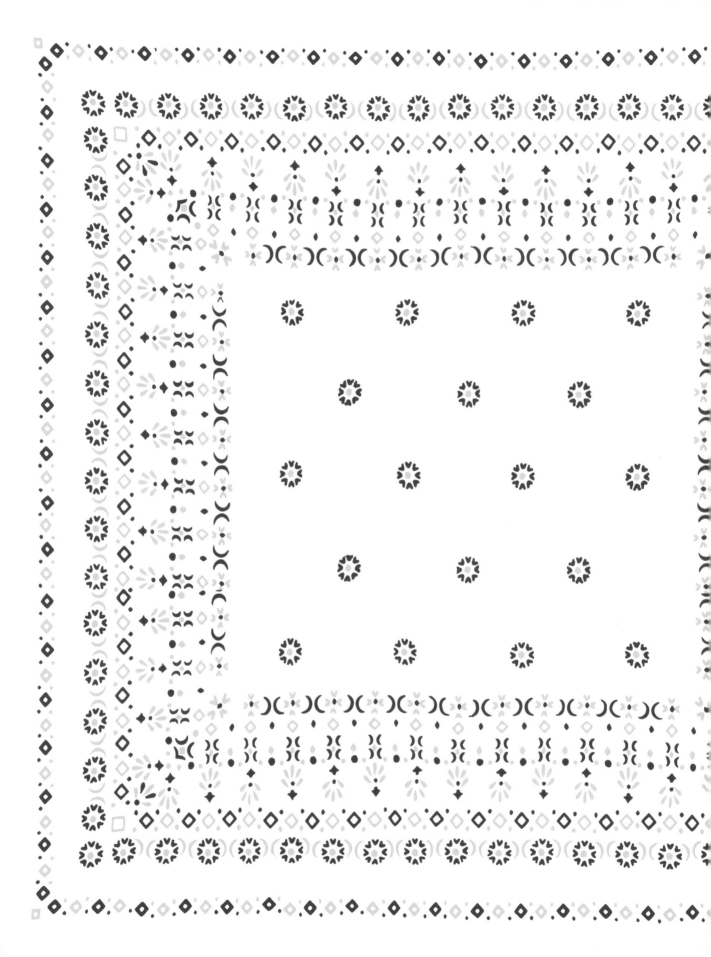

FABRIC, PATTERN, COLOR

CANVAS

CANVAS is a material you probably run into on a daily basis without even realizing it, whether it's an overnight duffel bag you own or a vintage painting on stretched canvas or, of course, your Converse high tops. ★ It's a great material to use in an interior setting because it's so durable and can be made water-resistant or even waterproof, which means you can use it as a shower curtain. Canvas can also be used for upholstery. It's inexpensive, tough and comes in lots of colors.

GINGHAM

Gingham can be used as a neutral, and you can layer on the patterns, especially when they're medium scale. Black and white is a classic color combo, but don't ignore blue-and-white, red-and-black, and green-and-white gingham. ★ As the saying goes, use every crayon in the box.

The pillow shams are from the 150-year-old Minnesota-based Faribault Woolen Mill. Using king-size bed shams is a simple trick to get bigger throw pillows. The plug-in pendant light from Schoolhouse Electric makes a handy reading light. The rug is from Mexico.

When I designed this basement remodel there was
no way to reroute the HVAC duct, so I painted it Benjamin
Moore Ballet Slippers pink and called it a day.

PLAID

A set of vintage balloon molds from Pacific Northwest retailer City Home is 3D art that repeats the plaid motif.

The Roman window shade fabric matches the bench cushion in this guest room lookout. The paint color is Farrow & Ball De Nimes, inspired by denim workwear.

I bought fabric shirting yardage from the Pendleton Woolen Mill store and used it for drapery as well as upholstery for this vintage chair.

There was a sunroom in this historic house I decorated for a family of Girl Scouts and guitar-playing model-train enthusiasts. I added a denim sofa, and the family uses it as a music and game room.

DENIM

FLORALS

FLORALS bring the outdoors in. They work in country homes, where they emphasize the indoor-outdoor flow, and in city homes, where they give you a taste of nature in your fifth-floor walk-up. You can introduce floral artwork or flowery furniture, such as a tulip table or an inlaid chest of drawers.

This wallpaper was inspired by the California poppy. It's bold, large scale and not precious. The fact that it's unexpected makes it modern. It was designed by my friend Alexis Hartman of Lake August. She does original paintings and translates them into wallpapers, so they have an artisan aspect. The paper is hand printed in the USA by a local printing mill. People see the dark background and think it's going to make the room dark. In this case it works, because it was the perfect amount, above a high wainscot, with natural light flowing in from the side.

HAIR-ON
HIDE

Layering hide rugs is handy for odd-shaped furniture arrangements as in this room, which I designed for a modern condo project in downtown Portland. Round 'em up!

L E A T H E R

Sometimes you've got to put in the work to break in a leather chair. It's like a baseball mitt: the more you use it, the more it molds to you. ★ Leather can be used in so many ways. It's a material that gets better with age. And it's family friendly, especially if you're okay with scuffs and nicks and water spots and literal elbow grease—all of which add character. ★ It's fine to mix leather colors. Maybe it's counterintuitive and seems like a design rule you can't break, but I think black and brown leather look great together, especially if one of the elements is vintage. This is harder to pull off in an outfit; black boots and a brown leather belt might look dorky. But again, rules are there to be broken. If you've got style, you can pull anything off.

OPPOSITE: This was a ground-up build in Bend, Oregon.
All the upholstery was made in North Carolina by Lee Industries.

OLIVE GREEN

The paint on these bookshelves is Tate Olive by Benjamin Moore, a favorite shade for casework.

RED, WHITE & BLUE

RED, WHITE AND BLUE can be a red chair, a blue sofa and a white wall, or a red, white and blue rug. Obviously, we associate red, white and blue with the American flag, but, history aside, they're simply nice colors that look good together. ☆ You can go super primary or more muted. So, red, white and blue can mean navy, maroon and cream or it can be turquoise, ruby and pearl. As an Americana maximalist, I use red, white and blue the way someone else uses taupe and beige.

The bench seat upholstery is a Sunbrella outdoor fabric, so it's kid and pet friendly.

SUMMER
STRIPES

ZEBRAS WEAR THEM, but so did nineteenth-century criminals. Stripes can relate to the beach or the lake or the cabin. ★ Big stripes, little stripes, ticking stripes, stripes on stripes—the more the merrier.

TEXTILES

Textiles are where I bring in pattern. ☆ Go ahead and mix florals with plaids, stripes and textures like corduroy, wool and denim. Pillows look best when they've literally been thrown on the sofa. Just please don't karate chop them.

Xs & Os

XS: Whether a cross or an X or a plus sign, it's a graphic motif that looks like a doodle to me. It's a symbol I've always associated with the last letter of my name, but people have all sorts of associations with it. It pops up even when you're not looking for it, in art and nature. It has great significance in Native American iconography. And in texting culture, it's a simple way of signing off with a kiss. In this guest bathroom, I sourced inexpensive black and white four-inch-square tiles for the shower walls and had them installed in a cross pattern. It's a lot of look for not a lot of money.

AND . . .

OS: Polka dots are a motif I go back to even if I'm not being intentional about it. They can be painted on the walls of a kid's room or painted on a floor. A collection of vintage dice on a bookshelf is a way to employ polka dots without being too literal. It's good to balance out a sharp-angled room with something circular. I ordered a random assortment of polka-dotted backsplash tile from Tempest Tileworks and arranged the tiles on the floor before the installer stuck them on the walls.

The rug is from my own collection with Thayer Design Studio, whose rugs are milled in Rhode Island. The bed, chair and dresser are vintage finds.

STICK 'EM UP

MAPS

MAPS AND CLASSROOM CHARTS, especially the old pull-down ones, cover
a lot of wall space and have a graphic punch. You don't have to frame
maps, which can be cost prohibitive. You just put a nail in the wall, stick
up a map and you're done. ★ You can buy vintage-style map holders (or
make them yourself), but you can also just hang them and let the bottoms
curl up. ★ Maps and charts cover a wide range of subjects, like botany,
astronomy, biology and, of course, travel. You can use them to honor an
artistic interest or a bucket-list destination.

CLOCKS

What's a more American experience than sitting in school and staring at the clock, waiting for class to end? ★ IBM clocks were manufactured in the '40s, became popular in the '60s, and were widely used in schools and libraries. You can find them at vintage stores or buy reproductions that actually work. ★ They're great for telling time, obviously. But they're also big graphic elements that act like kinetic sculptures in their own right.

Both of these clocks are from Schoolhouse Electric and are battery operated, which means you don't have to reset them when the power goes out.

PANORAMIC

I DON'T LIKE FAMILY PHOTOS IN THE ENTRY OF A HOUSE. They're more suited to private spaces, like the hallway to your bedroom. Yard longs work well in public spaces. They're conversational and unsentimental, the grumpy decorator's version of family photos. ★ Hanging just one of these is sort of precious, though it's fine if it's a particularly important photo that was handed down to you. If they're random strangers, they look better as a grouping. There are unconventional places these can go, such as over a door or under a window. They also look nice in a hallway, where they emphasize a linear space. ★ Yard longs that have been stuck in a shipping tube can benefit from being professionally framed. Matting will make them bigger and create space where your eye can rest. ★ Some of these go back as far as the 1920s. At that time, given camera technology, everyone had to sit still. You can find yard longs of military squadron reunions, plumber conventions and electric company union picnics. From a distance they're abstract, but when you get up close, you can see the stitching on people's jackets and what kind of shoes they're wearing. A lot of them are World War II era, so I often think about where these people ended up. No one's smiling in these—I mean, it's a company picnic!—but that's part of their charm.

PHOTOS

These are part of my own collection of panoramics that I've scavenged over the years.

FLAGS

For instant Americana, just add a flag.

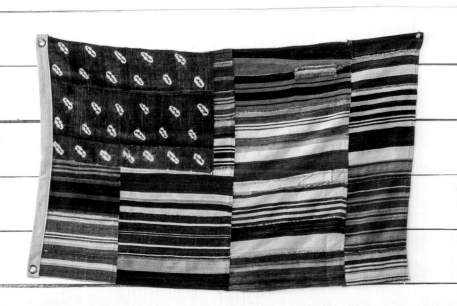

If you ever see a vintage porcelain Rexall Drug sign, don't leave the store without it.

SIGNS & BANNERS

OLD SIGNS usually have a story behind them. You can find manufacturing signs from factories that say things like "Don't Touch" or "Danger: High Voltage!" ☆ Drug store signs are common finds, as are food, hospitality and advertising ones. You might see a locksmith sign in the shape of a key, or a ginger ale sign in the shape of a bottle. They come in porcelain, painted wood, neon, tin and enamel, and you can collect them based on content, color or message. You can put a sign in a kitchen if it's topical (if it has something to do with, say, chickens or strawberries). ☆ Pennants, banners and camp flags are other examples of signage that add color and a message. I've put a banner that said "Raise Hell, Kid" in a tween's room.

Buffalo, New York–based Oxford Pennant designs and manufactures old-style pennants and banners out of felt. I collaborated with them on this custom camp flag.

BOTANICALS

**Tacking up a series of botanical prints
is an unfussy way to add interest to a blank
wall. The vintage Coleman lantern was
rewired as a bedside table lamp.**

THRIFTING

BASKETS

BASKETMAKING is a craft that's global. You can buy baskets made from Appalachian ash and you can buy baskets of woven grass made in East Africa. You can buy traditional Native American baskets reflecting regional styles directly from the artisans. And they all can live in the same room with a French laundry basket. ✴ Baskets are convenient bookshelf space fillers. They can be used as storage for sweaters and shoes in a bedroom or for an extra blanket in a guest room. They can store the toilet paper in a bathroom. You can put one on your coffee table to keep the remote in. (It's nice to put your remote away and even nicer to put it in a cool vintage basket.)

CANS & CONTAINERS

RETRO TINS HAD A RANGE OF THEMES from food storage to motor oil.
I tend to gravitate toward ones that are products I consume myself,
like potato chips. I don't use them for food storage but put them on the
shelf as decorative elements. You might find a vintage ten-pound tin
of butterscotch cookies that would have lasted a year for some family.
They're a good daily reminder to buy less and buy better.

I designed this custom credenza to hold a vinyl record collection for some informal clients who use their formal living room as a music room.

OPPOSITE: Chicken dishes bought at auction. I don't know what they are or what they're for, but I had to have them. Those chicken dishes are a line in the sand; you're either with me or against me.

COLLECTIONS

THREE OF ANYTHING IS A COLLECTION.

CROCKS & STONEWARE

Red Wing pottery is an American stoneware popularized by a company founded in 1877 in Red Wing, Minnesota. It's something you start to notice at vintage stores and antique malls. Collectors nerd out on the condition and the numbers, which refer to their gallon capacity. You can use them as planter pots, catchalls, umbrella stands, firewood holders or a bazillion other uses.

CROSS-STITCH

CROSS-STITCH SAMPLERS can be found inexpensively at vintage stores but might also be sold at auction houses for tens of thousands of dollars, depending on provenance. ★ I collect them in categories—by the pattern, the color or the message. These are all about friendship and feeling welcome. (Though I also like tongue-in-cheek ones, like "Quit Yer Bitchin'!") ★ Needlework is a category of art and design that when taken out of context can assume a modern sensibility.

Old Friends
Are True Friends

Welcome, Friends

OH WHAT A PLEASANT SIGHT IT IS
TO SEE THE FRUITFUL CLUSTER
BOWING DOWN THE TREE

Come Dear Friend
come here
and rest
You'll always be
A welcome
Guest

O LET MY NAME ENGRAVEN
STAND
BOTH ON THY HEART AND ON THY
HAND
SEAT ME UPON THINE ARM AND
WEAR
THAT PLEDGE OF LOVE FOREVER
THERE

PITCHERS & POTS

I prefer to drink orange juice right from the carton, whereas a pitcher makes a perfect flowerpot.

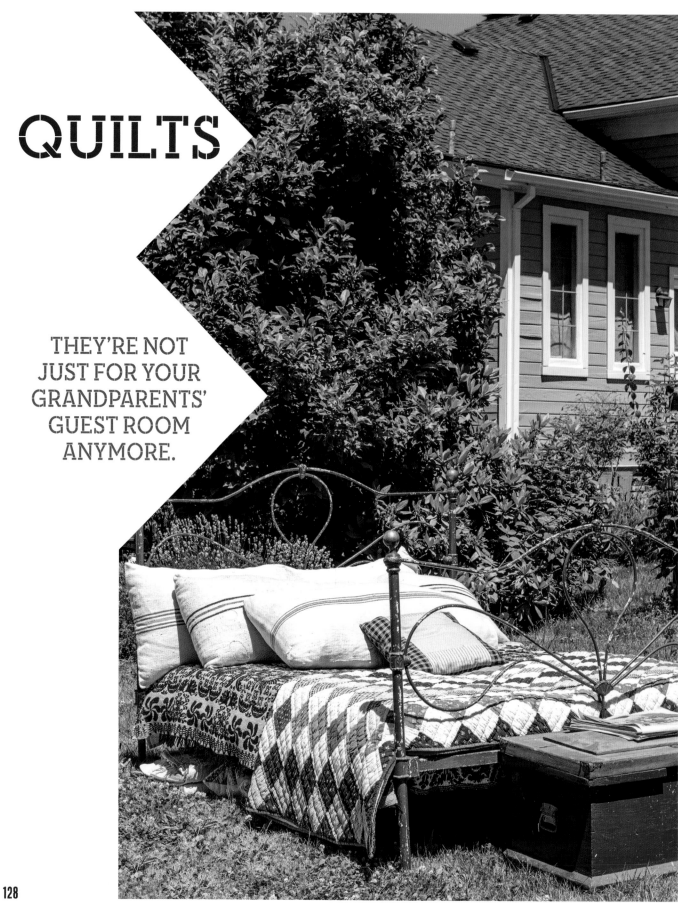

QUILTS

THEY'RE NOT JUST FOR YOUR GRANDPARENTS' GUEST ROOM ANYMORE.

FOLK ART

THIS ENTRYWAY FEATURES A COLLECTION OF FOLK ART PIECES,
including the no-frills Shaker broom, the handcrafted picnic basket, the embroidered welcome sign, the green stool made of reclaimed wood and the array of tramp art frames. Tramp art was made by amateurs using found objects like popsicle sticks, cigar boxes, pine cones and bits of wood. The rug is my own design, inspired by woven camp bracelets.

EAT,
DRINK,
VISIT

BARS & BAR CARTS

THE FIRST WESTERN SALOONS were established in the early 1800s, but people have found a way to bring a bit of that spirit into their own homes. You can create a fully functional wet bar with an ice maker, beverage fridge and sink, or you can just get a vintage bar cart and style it with some retro seltzer bottles and a table lamp. ★ Bar carts are movable and fun to decorate. They can be used for the purpose they were designed for, or not. Even if you're not using it for its intended purpose, a bar cart can be handy for rolling storage or for offering dessert and coffee after a dinner party. ★ Whether you're serving whiskey or milkshakes, bars and bar carts create something for people to gather around.

ABOVE: The clients I designed for wanted a gathering space adjacent to the TV area so people could bop over and sit at the bar, or the homeowners could make a drink and take it back to the sofa. The bar is oak; the upper cabinet has chicken wire instead of glass. The backsplash has mirrored tiles, which is a modern take on an old-fashioned bar with a giant mirror behind it that would twinkle when the lights hit it at night.

OPPOSITE: The *Nothing* photo is by Seattle landscape photographer Paul Edmondson. This is from his series of billboards taken throughout the American West.

COOLERS

The furniture on the porch all comes from Minnesota-based Loll, which designs and makes sustainable but super durable outdoor furniture from recycled milk jugs. In wet regions, teak furniture doesn't stand up to the elements. Investing a bit in this category of furniture means you won't have to keep buying stuff every summer.

THERE'S A COOLER IN EVERY VINTAGE STORE. Sometimes I'll buy one just to carry the other stuff I buy. Now I have a wall of coolers in my garage. They're my version of the carryout bag. ★ Coolers are handy for what they're supposed to be used for, i.e., cooling drinks. They're a good place to hide toys when your neighbors stop by, and their handles make them easy to move. A lot of them have bottle openers built onto them so you don't break your teeth trying to open a root beer bottle. ★ This turquoise cooler lives on my deck. I was wandering an antique mall when I saw a woman walk in and put it down in her booth. I immediately grabbed it. She told me it had been her grandmother's and that it was what they used for camping. She seemed relieved to meet the person who was buying it. She opened it for me and showed me the tray and how clean everything was kept. She was like a proud owner handing over the keys.

TABLECLOTHS

The wallpaper in this breakfast room features geese in flight by L.A.–based Lake August. I grabbed these amaranth cuttings at the farmers market because they remind me of a Muppet.

There seems to be a school of thought on tablecloths that they're more formal if they go to the floor. Shorter tablecloths are casual and your knees fit underneath.

The pillowcases are 1930s sugar sacks. The patterned drapery is actually outdoor fabric, so it won't fade from the sun hitting it. I had to use a swag clip for the pendant light because the electrical box was off-center.

GRAIN
&
FLOUR
SACKS

VINTAGE GRAIN SACKS are made from a really heavyweight linen that's indestructible, so you can drag them around your house or take them outside. A lot of them come from Europe, and they have different stripe patterns to indicate who the farmer was or what was inside them. ★ You can make great body pillows from the really long ones. I stuff them with down inserts so they can be molded and smashed like a Tempur-Pedic. Usually one side is sewn and one open; I keep them that way so I can add or remove inserts as needed. I've seen them pulled over the backs of dining chairs as sort of makeshift slipcovers. They were useful for something specific at one point and now they're being used for something else, which is a form of recycling. Grain and flour sacks have an American farmhouse look, but their function is universal.

142

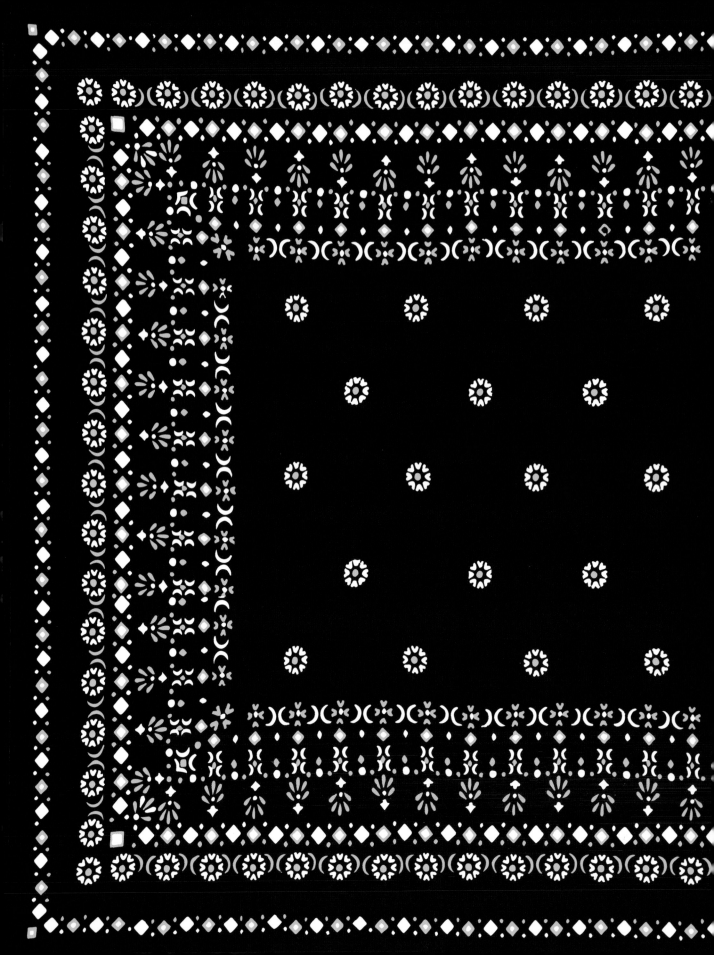

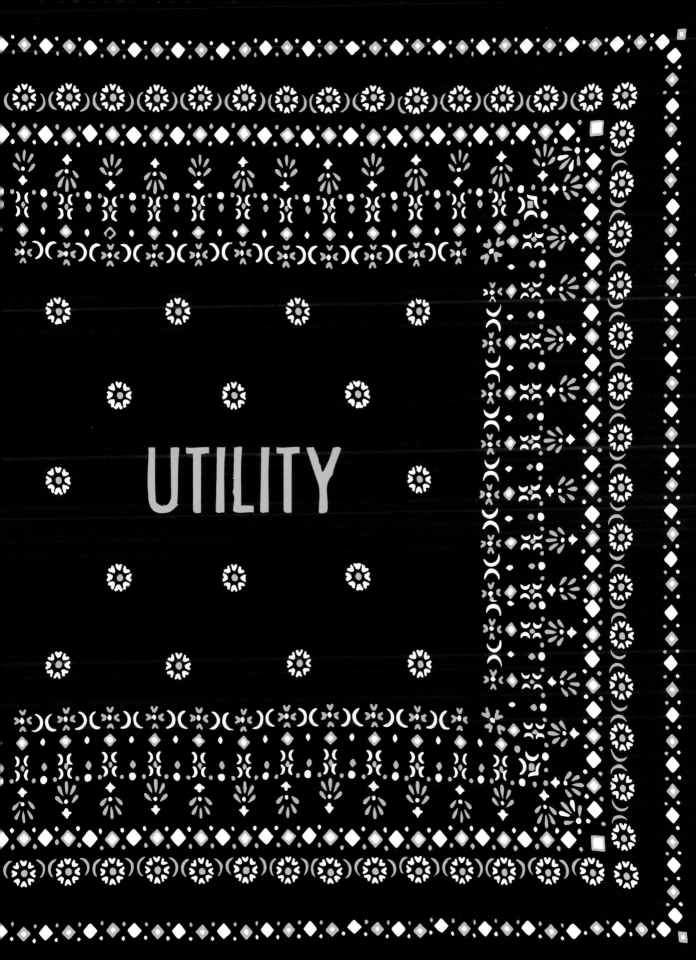

UTILITY

TRUNKS

ANY PIECE OF FURNITURE that can do two things is helpful, and vintage trunks are a perfect example of that. Most of us have found one in the attic at one point or another, where it might have been used to store old Halloween costumes or family albums or the *National Geographic* collection someone couldn't bear to get rid of. Use one as a coffee table, place it at the foot of a bed, or throw it in the back of the SUV instead of luggage on your next vacation for a nostalgic road-trip vibe.

A graphic Woolrich blanket dresses up an antique pew sourced from Urbanite in Southeast Portland, a favorite hunting ground for vintage finds.

MUDROOMS
YOU CAN TELL A LOT ABOUT A FAMILY BY WHAT'S HANGING ON THEIR MUDROOM HOOKS

Windbreakers are easy to grab for morning walks on the sand in a coastal Oregon beach house.

There's room for a family of seven to kick off their snow boots and store their winter jackets and ski goggles in this L-shaped utility space.

PLEASE WASH HANDS

Several kids can crowd around this double cast-iron wall-mounted Kohler sink in my clients' upstairs bathroom. The tile pattern was inspired by a vintage trade blanket. I had to source the tiles from a couple of different vendors to get the colors right.

"FARMHOUSE" refers to the way these sinks are installed with the exposed apron. They can work in a rustic, traditional or modern space, depending on the kitchen. These were designed to be big before there was running water. They're also good for giving your newborn a bath. ★ Pedestal sinks are a handy choice in a powder room; they're sculptural and space saving. You still see them sometimes in old-fashioned hotel rooms that have a sink. The old ones are cast iron with a porcelain finish. The hot and cold faucets were spread out so you wouldn't clunk your head when you were washing your hair.

ABOVE: The Lucite desk in this upstairs loft is transparent, so you can still appreciate the setting.

OPPOSITE: This home didn't have room for a separate office, so a sunny corner of the kitchen provides a spot to perch and check emails. The painted stool was reupholstered with a vintage grain sack. The teddy bear was mine when I was a baby.

You can dedicate an entire room as a home office, or you can just carve out a corner of your kitchen. All you really need is a comfy flour-sack stool and a flat surface for your coffee cup. Surround yourself with stuff you love so work doesn't feel like work.

WORK FROM
HOME

ROPE

ROPE is a universal and versatile design material. It brings to mind everything from sailing to swings to Indiana Jones's lasso. ★ Rope detailing can be highly nautical, ultra-western or super rustic. Some traditional ways to use it include as upholstery or as an accent material—a rope-covered cabinet handle, for instance. ★ The handmade aspect of rope objects reminds me of knitting. ★ There's something organic about rope that can bring a modern space back to earth.

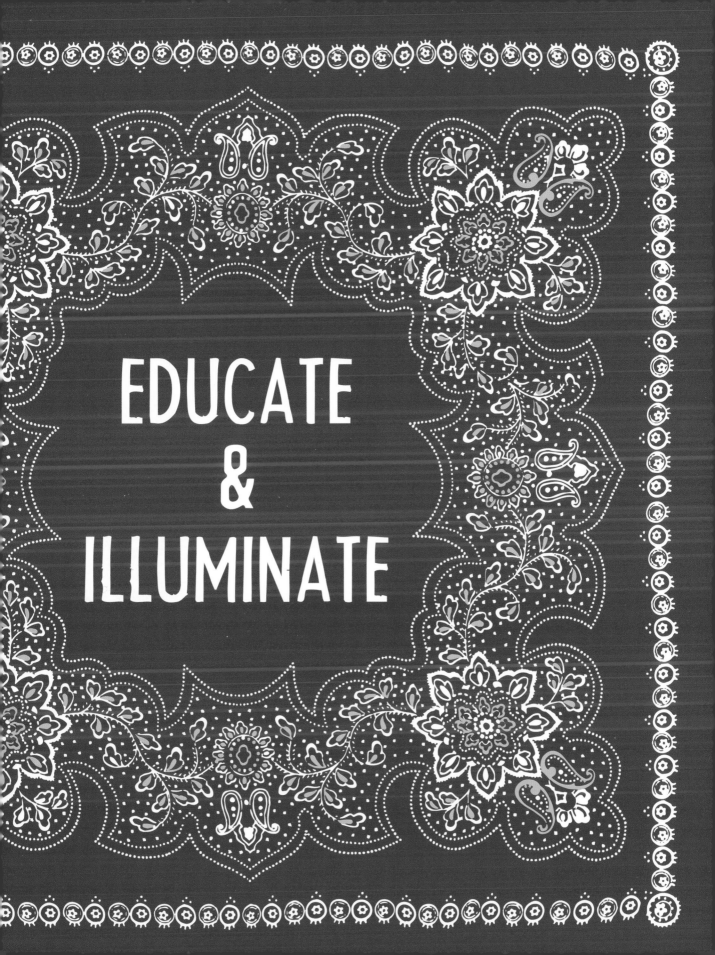

The 1960s lamp was
an eBay find. The
woven strips of ceramic
resemble spaghetti.

VINTAGE LIGHTING

You can make a lamp out of anything. There are pottery lamps and industrial lamps and even lamps made from trombones. ★ Vintage lighting is a category that can give any space character. Whether it's a table lamp or a pendant over a breakfast table, lamps can bring a pop of color or an interesting shape to an otherwise square space.

PAINT BY

A LOT OF US REMEMBER paint by numbers from when we were kids. There are a ton of landscapes and seascapes. I stay away from the clowns, but I like the animal ones a lot.

The lounge chair is a new design from Loll, inspired by a motel chair from the 1940s. It's made from steel and recycled plastic. A picnic basket can serve as a side table in a pinch.

BOOKS & BOOKSHELVES

A ROOM IS NOT A ROOM WITHOUT A STACK OF BOOKS.

The shelves in both these rooms are made from maple plywood, with the lower cubby sections designed to fit a one-bushel Steele Canvas basket. The gallery wall references travel, nature and America's national parks. The Eagle Patrol piece is a vintage camp sign for a Boy Scout troop.

This home was a new build for a family outside of Boston. I designed the cabinetry around a niche for the sofa. The bookshelves were installed first, so when the sofa was delivered it was a real nail-biter until I knew it fit.

FIREPLACES
& FIRE PITS

The white folding camp chairs are vintage. I had them reupholstered in a reversible outdoor Pendleton fabric called Harding, one of the company's most popular designs.

The brick fireplace was the only architectural detail kept intact after this beach house renovation. The white pottery lamp was made by Charlie West, a potter based in Georgia. The eagle sculpture on the mantel is cast iron, from 1915. The molded-plywood Eames lounge chair is an uncomfortable design icon.

Freestanding Malm fireplaces have been designed and manufactured in Northern California since the 1960s. In this space, the fireplace takes on a campfire aesthetic.

HISTORY & NOSTALGIA

AIRSTREAM

THIS MAY BE OBVIOUS, but there are no right angles in an Airstream. ★ This trailer was a project for a coffee brand's mobile coffee shop. It wasn't meant for overnight camping. I had to come up with materials that could incorporate the curves plus practicalities like electrical. Cork is a great underused flooring option: it's mold resistant and soft. The built-ins are maple plywood with laminate fronts. I used outdoor fabric for the cushions. ★ I wanted to speak to coffee and mobile camping and road trips, so it's fitted out with framed artwork of states, vintage coffee mugs and enamelware coffeepots. Everything had to do double duty, so the seating has slider doors for storage underneath. There's no wasted space. ★ It was a dream project. Not only was it this awesome piece of Americana, it was coffee related. I don't have an office outside of my home, so I bounce around town doing this coffee-shop musical chairs. All my design work is fueled by coffee.

BANDANAS

I was working with a client who said it would be cool to have a bandana print for a room we wanted to wallpaper. When I went to the wallpaper store, though, I found nothing like that existed, so I collaborated with a graphic designer to take bits and pieces from some of my own vintage bandanas then found a Chicago-based printer to manufacture it. It took a year, so we had to finish the client's project using something else and I installed it in my home office.

WHEN YOU COLLECT BANDANAS, you start to have your favorites. For me, the more beat-up and sun worn the better. I look for the Elephant brand, which is considered the original Americana bandana. Keep your eyes out for bandanas with the elephant trunk facing down; it means they could have been made before 1950. ★ These are framed in a cool setting and grouped for effect, but you can also keep one in your back pocket to wipe your nose or clean oatmeal off your kid's shirt. ★ Framing a bandana is an easy DIY. Just steam it then use fabric glue or sew it right onto a board. Using matting gives it some breathing room behind the frame. When hung on a gallery wall it can look like an abstract arrangement, almost like pointillism with just a bunch of patterns in blue; but when you get up close, you appreciate the details. ★ Not a lot of fashion accessories can go from West Virginia coal miners to Rosie the Riveter to spaghetti western cowboys. I even used them as inspiration for wallpaper. Bandanas are at home everywhere.

WILD WEST

Growing up, I idolized Ralph Lauren, who was another East Coast, middle-class Jewish kid obsessed with the American West. His was the most aspirational brand out there. While other kids were playing cowboys and Indians, I was pretending to be Ralph Lifshitz selling handmade neckties to my school friends.

The cowboy painting is from the '30s or '40s and was an online shopping score. The American flag pillow is needlepoint, another Americana mainstay. The Schoolhouse Electric sconce simply plugs into an outlet; here's it's both a picture light and a reading lamp.

An old toy crate is covered in an appealing vintage ranch-scene wallpaper. It serves as a bedside table as well as a storage bin. The walls wear the white colorway of my bandana wallpaper.

The futon upholstery is a design that honors Chief Joseph.
It was first woven by Pendleton in the 1920s.

PENDLETON

Just hearing the name immediately conjures visions of their blankets. Based in Portland, Oregon, the company has been around since the 1860s. There are very few operating woolen mills in the U.S. today, but Pendleton still manufactures products in Oregon and Washington. ✭ Whether you use the wool for upholstery projects or drape a throw over the arm of a couch, the bold patterns and primary colors of their fabrics bring a piece of the Pacific Northwest to any room. ✭ Using Pendleton is a good exercise in how to mix patterns. A little goes a long way, but a lot goes a really long way.

The brass stag towel hooks from Rejuvenation hold a variety of patterned Pendleton towels in an outdoor hot tub area.

SUMMER CAMP VIBES

IT MIGHT SEEM like plaids and stripes don't go together, but when they're medium scale and you're decorating a room in a summer-camp style, they can mix. You can also get sort of matchy, which is not something I normally do, but you can get away with it in a themed room. ☆ There are lots of ways to play up camp style. Was it John Muir who said peanut M&Ms make good slingshot ammo?

The deco-inspired Springer chair dates back to the early midcentury and was manufactured by Heywood-Wakefield, a U.S. furniture company founded in 1897 that's still around today. It takes on new life with an outdoor jacquard fabric. The best part of this chair is the ebonized armrests; they've been stripped by 70 years of elbow grease.

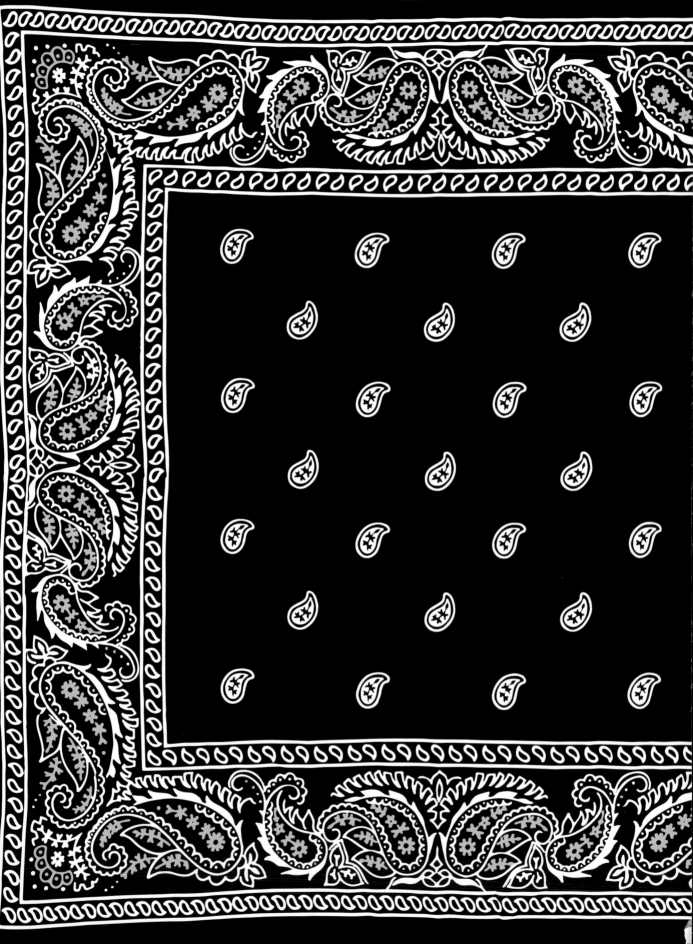

The "Free the Sardines"
wallpaper is by
L.A.–based designer
Clare Vivier.

ANIMALS

REFERENCING LOCAL WILDLIFE in modern interiors is a way of honoring the landscape. Deer, raccoons, pheasants and bison might at some time cross paths in reality, so mixing them together in a room becomes a subtle nod to locale. To me, it would be weird to mix in a tiger here, since there are no tigers in Central Oregon. (There are no bison either, but this footstool from Old Hickory reminds us that there once were.)

COTS
& TENTS

I love traditional tents made out of army duck canvas. This one is from Denver Tent, which has been making tents in Colorado since 1890. The cot cushions are all covered in fabrics inspired by Pendleton's national park blanket stripes.

CANVAS feels so much nicer than nylon, but it's heavy. You wouldn't carry traditional tents on your backpack. The canvas ones are for car camping or the lawn. ★ You can use them as a kids' playhouse or a backyard sunshade, like an extra little covered porch. I like the comforts. I fill mine up with quilts, my Coleman cooler and a lantern. ★ A camp cot is a great addition to your tent setup, but if you buy a nice one it can go in the hallway of an office or home. I like to have cushions made so you can mix and match patterns and colors. ★ Camp cots fold up really easily, so when you pack up to go home from your campsite or the beach, you just shake off the dirt and graham cracker crumbs.

I had a skirted cushion made for a guest room nap spot.

GREENERY

You can make a big statement with any plants and clippings from your yard. Just don't overthink the composition. I stick to one plant variety: maple leaves, olive branches, quince. You can buy them at a specialty store or steal them from your neighbor's garden, like Peter Rabbit.

Clients asked me to decorate their basement workout room. I have no interest in exercise equipment, so I wanted to make it a greenhouse. The room has floor-to-ceiling windows, so it seemed like the perfect place for a wall full of houseplants.

The small entry table adds a spot for cut branches and space shuttles in a client's historic home. The stools are by midcentury furniture designer Paul McCobb; I found them at a sidewalk sale.

LOGS, STICKS & TWIGS

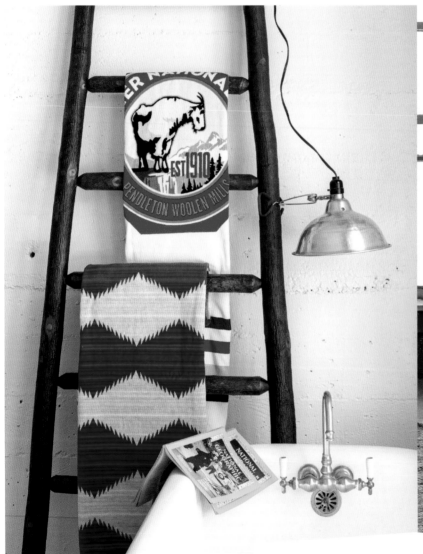

Here I use Old Hickory's blanket ladder as a towel holder. Their Leanback Chair was originally designed in the 1930s. Once you sit in it, you won't want to get out. The pedestal table features a reclaimed top.

There's something about furniture that looks just as good indoors as outdoors, and exposed-wood or log furniture is the best example. Upholster it for a more modern look inside, or leave the seats raw or with caning for the porch. If you're feeling ambitious, take a walk through the woods then make your own using fallen branches.

TAXIDERMY

I was the passenger in a car the night before my high school graduation when we hit a deer. My friends and I were the designated drivers, so it's ironic that we were the ones to get in an accident. Since then, I've been a little squirrelly about decorating with real animals. ★ I designed this vacation home from the ground up for a family with five kids. We wanted that mountain-house look, so I reached out to artist Chase Halland of Faraway Lovely in Idaho, who makes the stag busts out of foam, covers them in Pendleton wool, and then adds vintage and found antlers. I thought it would be cool to do one for each kid, so we went through all the fabrics and picked ones that would look good together. This is a modern way to use taxidermy and honor the deer as an animal. It's also a way to get some pattern onto a white wall. The busts work well in an entry or a mudroom since you can use the antlers as a hat rack.

MAX HUMPHREY is an interior designer, art director and stylist based in Portland, Oregon. Originally from New Hampshire, Max attended college in Boston then moved to Los Angeles to work in TV and film production. After touring the U.S. and England as the bass player in a punk rock band signed to a major record label, he discovered a passion for interior design. Max has designed suburban homes, estates on the historic registry, coastal mansions and beach shacks, modern downtown condos, log cabins, a ski-bum hideaway, winery tasting rooms, a hipster dental office, retail stores, a podcast studio, an Airstream trailer, and a food truck for a burger joint. He's a sought-after art director for retail catalogs and has created campaigns for local home décor brands and global big box stores. Max has a line of American-made wool rugs and a wallpaper collection, and his projects have appeared in all the fancy design magazines. Max was named one of *Country Living*'s "100 Most Creative People." www.maxhumphrey.com.

CHASE REYNOLDS EWALD is the author of eleven books on architecture, interior design, traditional craftsmanship and cooking. A graduate of Yale and the Graduate School of Journalism at Berkeley, Chase has written and photographed for many publications. A blogger and regular contributor to *Mountain Living*, she is also Senior Editor of *Western Art & Architecture Magazine* and the Design Columnist for *Big Sky Journal*. Chase's book *American Rustic*, one of many collaborations with photographer Audrey Hall, was named one of the Best Home Design Books by *Architectural Digest*. Her recent book *Inspired by Place* is a monograph on the work of CLB Architects. *Bison: An American Icon* is a portrait of America's national mammal. www.chasereynoldsewald.com.

CHRISTOPHER DIBBLE is a West Coast–based photographer specializing in lifestyle, interiors and portraiture. His work has been featured in *House Beautiful*, *Architectural Digest Spain*, *Dwell*, *HGTV*, *Country Living*, *Entertainment Weekly*, and *People Magazine*. Clients have included Sunbrella, The Shade Store, Framebridge and many designers, artists, and architects. Dibble has been profiled in *Popular Photography Magazine* and was named one of *The Advocate's* "40 under 40." A graduate of Art Center College of Design, he works to combine his understanding of both portraiture and interior design to create images that tell a story. www.christopherdibble.com.